Surprising Snakes

By Leya Roberts

Celebration Press
Pearson Learning Group

Contents

Snake Basics

You may know a great deal about snakes. You've read about them in science books, and maybe you've seen snakes in your yard or while camping. Perhaps you've watched them in zoos.

So why learn more? The best reason is that snakes are fascinating! There are many things that the average person doesn't know about snakes. Here's your chance to learn some surprising facts. But first, think about what you already know.

A garter snake strikes only when threatened.

You know what snakes look like. Though snakes vary in size, they have long, usually thin bodies and no legs. Snakes slither along on their bellies and flick out forked tongues. Their bodies are very flexible, so they can bend in almost every direction.

You've probably learned that snakes are **vertebrates**; that is, they have backbones. They are also **reptiles**, which means they breathe air (not water), have scaly skin, and are **ectothermic**, or "cold-blooded." Being ectothermic means that an animal's body temperature depends on the temperature of its surroundings. A snake cannot produce its own body heat inside. If the air around a snake is cold, the snake's body temperature will be cold. To warm up, it needs to go someplace warmer—into the sunshine on a warm rock, for example.

Maybe you've seen snakes in the wild before. Snakes live almost everywhere. They live in forests, fields, and swamps. They live on mountains, underground, and in tropical rain forests where it is warm and damp. But they usually can't live where it is extremely cold, like Antarctica. This, as you can probably guess, is because they are ectothermic. Snakes can't warm up if the temperature around them is constantly below freezing.

For most snakes the best temperature is about 85°F. When it is very cold, snakes' bodies slow down, and they can hardly move. To get warmer, snakes move around and change their position often.

Only a few snakes can survive in very cold areas. Many snakes **hibernate**, or go into a sleeplike state, in caves, dens, or underground burrows for up to eight of the coldest months. For warmth many snakes often share the same den.

So what else is there to know? Lots! The basic information about snakes is interesting enough, but the specific ways that snakes look, eat, and protect themselves are even more amazing!

Most boa constrictors live in tropical areas of South America.

A Snake's Body

A snake's body looks rather simple; it is long and usually thin like a garden hose. In fact, snakes' bodies are much more complex than they look. They have many unique features that have helped snakes to adapt to many different environments.

A Head with a Tail?

Most snakes look like they are all head and tail. Snakes do have tails, but most of what you see is their bodies. You can tell the parts of a snake by looking at a snake skeleton.

Your ribs protect your heart and lungs. Snakes' ribs protect all of their organs, including their digestive tracts. Snakes' ribs, however, are not connected by a breastbone as human ribs are. Instead they are connected to the backbone by muscles. This structure allows snakes to wind, twist, and slither their bodies.

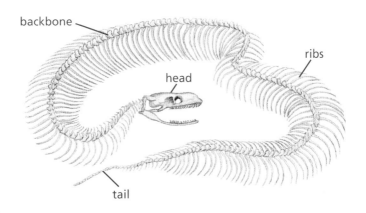

backbone

ribs

head

tail

In rare cases a snake has two heads. This happens particularly among king snakes and garter snakes. Each head has its own brain, so each head makes its own decisions. This sometimes causes problems. Sometimes the two heads fight each other over food, even though the food is going to the same stomach!

A two-headed king snake

Snake Legs

Snakes have no legs. The first snakes probably had hips and short legs like those of lizards, but their legs disappeared during their development over millions of years. However, pythons and boas still have two tiny claws called **spurs** near their tails, where their hips and legs once were.

Although spurs are useless for walking, scientists think that spurs show that snakes are closely related to lizards.

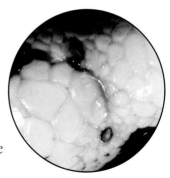

Spurs on the underside of a python near the tail

7

Scales

Like all reptiles, snakes have scaly bodies. What exactly are those scales made of? They're made mostly of a substance called **keratin**—the same material that forms your fingernails and the claws and hoofs of animals. These scales help protect snakes from injury and keep moisture in their bodies.

Snakes can have anywhere from 8 to 100 rows of scales covering their bodies from head to tail. The scales overlap like shingles on a roof. This arrangement allows the snake's body to move easily.

Some snakes look slimy, but if you touch a snake, you'll feel cool, dry skin. It may feel smooth or rough, depending on the type of snake. Some snake skin looks wet because the scales are shiny. Other snakes have dull or prickly scales.

Don't Blink!

Did you ever notice that snakes don't blink? Their eyes are always open, even when they sleep. This is so because snakes don't have movable eyelids.

A clear scale called a spectacle covers a snake's eye.

8

Instead, snakes have an unusual way to keep the dust out of their eyes. They have a hard, clear scale called a **spectacle** that covers each eye. It's almost like a permanent contact lens, and it protects the snake's entire eye.

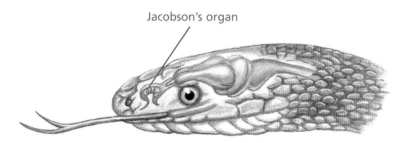

Jacobson's organ

Flicking Tongues

Snakes are known for flicking their tongues in and out of their mouths. That movement actually helps snakes' sense of smell.

Snakes flick out their tongues to pick up scent particles in the air or on the ground. In the roof of their mouths, their tongues brush across an organ of smell and taste called Jacobson's organ. A Jacobson's organ has two small holes, one for each fork in a snake's tongue. The organ then sends messages to the brain, which analyzes each scent. This information helps snakes identify and follow prey, such as a frog or a rat.

Growing, Growing, Grown?

Young snakes grow quickly, often becoming twice as large by the time they are a year old. Then, as they get older, their rate of growth slows down. Unlike humans and other animals, older snakes can still continue to grow throughout their lives.

Snakes have two main layers of skin. The inner layer is made up of growing cells. The thin outer layer is made up of dead cells, which protect the living cells below. New scales are always growing under the outer layer.

A snake molting

Several times a year, to make room for their growing bodies, snakes **molt**, or shed the thin outer layer of their skin. They molt when their skin becomes dried, loosened, and worn out. Just before molting, snakes usually become less active, their skin looks dull, and the spectacles over their eyes grow milky or bluish.

If you've ever found a snake's skin, you might have noticed that the covering for the whole body (including the spectacles over the eyes) was in one piece. But it was inside out!

Here's why. The shedding process starts at the snake's head. The snake finds something rough, like a tree or a rock, and rubs its face against it. It continues until the dried outer layer of skin is loosened and pushed down around its neck. As the snake wriggles forward out of its skin, the skin peels back and inside out—the way a sock might turn inside out if you peel it back from your ankle to your toes.

Large and Small

Snakes vary a great deal in size. Some pythons can be five times the length of a tall person—almost 33 feet. Anacondas can be about as long, but are much heavier and thicker around than pythons. Some anacondas weigh hundreds of pounds. The smallest snakes can be as short as a pencil and may be mistaken for worms.

Feeding Habits

Snakes are **carnivorous**; that is, they eat meat. Snakes eat insects, birds, fish, eggs, and even mammals, such as rabbits and pigs. Although some snakes eat their prey while it is still alive, most snakes kill their prey before eating it. With no legs to run and catch their prey, and no hands or paws to hold it, snakes have some interesting ways to find and catch a meal. How do they do it?

A Hug Before Eating

Many snakes are **constrictors**. They wait until a tasty animal approaches, grab it with their jaws, and wrap their bodies around and around it. Next they constrict—or squeeze—their prey tighter and tighter. Soon the animal stops breathing. Then they swallow the animal whole.

A constrictor squeezing its prey

Some Poisonous Snakes	Some Nonpoisonous Snakes
boomslang	anaconda
coral snake	ball python
cottonmouth	boa constrictor
king cobra	corn snake
Asian green pit viper	garter snake
rattlesnake	hognose snake

Venomous Snakes

Although most snakes are harmless to people, some snakes are poisonous. They use **venom**—a poison—to kill their prey. Venomous snakes have sacs of venom inside their cheeks. These sacs are connected to the snake's fangs by hollow tubes. The snake plunges its fangs into its prey and injects venom through the fangs. The amount of time varies among species, but usually in a few minutes the poison takes effect, and the prey dies.

A group of snakes called vipers have movable front fangs that fold back in their mouths when not in use. Their fangs are long and extremely sharp. When vipers are ready to strike, they open their mouths and the fangs spring forward, ready for action. The strike is quick, and the long fangs inject venom deeply into the prey. Adders and rattlesnakes are vipers.

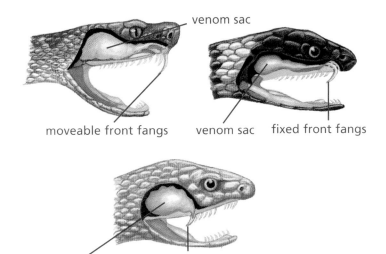

moveable front fangs

venom sac   fixed front fangs

venom sac   rear fangs

Another group of venomous snakes have fixed front fangs, which do not fold down but are always upright. Cobras and coral snakes belong to this group. Their fangs are somewhat shorter than those of vipers.

A third group have rear fangs in the upper jaw at the back of the mouth. Their fangs are grooved and short. African boomslang snakes and vine snakes have rear fangs.

Swallowing Prey

Snakes don't chew their food—they swallow it whole with their mouths open. Most snakes have hooklike teeth that point toward the backs of their mouths. Snakes use these teeth to help grip an animal as they work it down their throats.

Snakes produce lots of saliva while they are gulping down an animal. The saliva makes everything slippery, which helps the meal slide down from the mouth into the throat more easily.

A snake's mouth doesn't look particularly big, but snakes can swallow animals that are wider than their own heads. How do they do it?

Snakes' jaws have hinged bones that provide extra movement. Additionally, the **ligaments** that join the upper and lower jaws stretch like elastic. So do the ligaments that connect the lower jaws. This structure allows snakes to stretch their jaws widely apart. The snake's ribs also spread apart and allow the body to widen to make room for the prey.

Snakes that eat small prey, such as lizards and mice, swallow them in about 15 minutes. Those that eat large prey, such as deer and goats, often take more than an hour to swallow them.

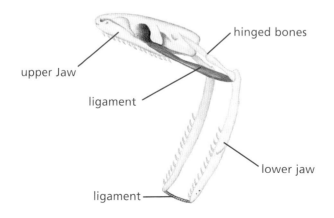

upper Jaw

hinged bones

ligament

lower jaw

ligament

An anaconda feeding on a caiman, a reptile similar to an alligator

Big Meals

The amount of food snakes need varies according to their size and how active they are. Some snakes are not very active, so they don't need to eat often. An average snake eats once every two weeks or so. Young snakes and smaller snakes eat more often. Bigger snakes may eat only five or six times a year. What about huge snakes? Pythons and anacondas have been known to survive for more than a year without eating.

Defenses Against Enemies

Snakes live in many different places and have many different enemies. Animals that eat snakes include wildcats, foxes, weasels, skunks, and eagles. Also among snakes' enemies are certain other snakes. For example, king snakes and king cobras frequently kill and eat other snakes.

The mongoose is known for its ability to kill snakes, especially cobras. Usually a mongoose doesn't attack a large cobra, but in a fight with one, the mongoose, with its speed and sharp teeth, will usually win.

Also well known for killing nonpoisonous and poisonous snakes is the African secretary bird. It jumps around a snake, hitting it again and again with the sharp claws on its feet.

This California king snake is eating another snake.

Bigger snakes have bigger enemies. Pythons, for example, might be attacked by panthers, alligators, or crocodiles. Certain snakes have unusual ways of defending themselves against these various enemies.

Rattling

The rattles at the end of a rattlesnake's tail may be the defense you know best. But what you might not know about rattlesnakes is that their rattles are *only* a defense. They rattle to scare away enemies, but not when they are stalking prey. If you think about it, this makes perfect sense. They don't want to alert their prey to their presence, so they hold their rattles still when stalking.

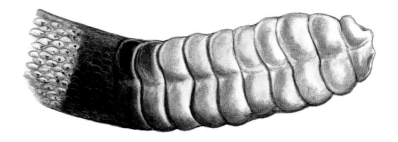

A rattlesnake makes a rattling sound by shaking
its rattle back and forth rapidly.

What's inside the rattle that makes that whirring, or buzzing sound? You might be surprised to learn that the rattles are hollow. They are made of segments of hard, thick scales joined together. The distinctive sound is made when the scaly segments of the rattle clack together while the snake shakes its tail.

A hognose snake playing dead to fool an enemy

Playing Dead

Since many animals prefer to eat live prey, some kinds of snakes play dead when approached by an enemy. The hognose snake, for example, flips over onto its back when an enemy is about to attack.

The hognose snake lies perfectly still. It puts its head back with its mouth open and its tongue hanging out. Then the enemy will likely leave it alone and continue its search for something live. When the enemy is gone, the hognose turns back over and crawls away.

Hissing

Snakes use sounds effectively to frighten their enemies. Most snakes hiss when they sense danger. They make this sound by forcing air through their windpipes.

One group of snakes called bullsnakes make an especially loud hiss. The sound is produced by a thin flap located in front of the windpipe. This flap vibrates when the snake forces air out of its windpipe.

Stinking!

Some snakes, such as garter snakes and grass snakes, put out a smelly substance to chase enemies away. Snakes release this liquid from an area near their tails. They have a variety of ways to use this smelly stuff.

Some snakes coil up and release the liquid, which then spreads over their own bodies. Enemies don't want to eat something that smells that bad!

Other snakes can spray stinky stuff over their attackers. This is often enough to make the predator leave—fast!

A spitting cobra can spray venom into an attacker's eyes.

Spitting

Some snakes spray venom at their enemies as a means of defense. When threatened, spitting cobras usually raise their head and the front part of their body and squirt jets of venom from tiny holes at the front of each fang tip. The venom flies through the air up to eight feet. The cobra aims right at its attacker's eyes.

Cobras have great aim and are often right on target. Getting hit with venom is very painful, so an enemy stops its attack to try to clear its eyes. Cobra venom is so strong it can blind an animal (or a human).

A herpetologist observes an emerald tree boa.

Snake Experts

You now know more about snakes than most people do. But there is even more to learn about these interesting animals!

If you are fascinated by snakes, you might want to think about becoming a **herpetologist**. A herpetologist studies reptiles and amphibians and observes, measures, and tests them. The word *herpetology* comes from the Greek word *herpeton*, which means "crawling thing."

To learn more about snakes, you may wish to observe them in a zoo. Exhibits of large snakes are becoming especially popular.

You may also wish to observe snakes in the wild—since they live on every continent except Antarctica. If you do, be careful not to disturb them. Most will bite if they feel threatened. Even the bite of a nonpoisonous snake can cause a serious wound. Always observe snakes from a safe distance.

So impress your friends and startle your parents! Share what you know. Snakes are amazing, aren't they?

Glossary

carnivorous	meat-eating
constrictor	a snake that squeezes its prey to death
ectothermic	having a body temperature that depends on the temperature of its surroundings; also called "cold-blooded"
herpetologist	a scientist who studies reptiles and amphibians
hibernate	to go into a sleeplike state
keratin	a material that makes up scales, horns, hoofs, and other hard areas that grow outside an animal's body
ligament	a tough band of tissue that connects the ends of bones
molt	to shed the thin outer layer of skin
reptile	a member of a group of animals that breathe air, have scaly skin, and are ectothermic
spectacle	a hard, clear scale that covers each eye of a snake
spurs	two tiny claws near the tail of some snakes
venom	a poison produced by some animals, including snakes
vertebrate	an animal that has a backbone